Foreword

Jesus Christ is unique. He is the founder of the Christian faith, the centre point of time and the pivot of history. He has had a greater influence on civilisation than any other person who has ever lived. The Bible teaches us that he is the Second Person of the Eternal Trinity, the Son of the Living God. This same Jesus left the glory of heaven and came into the world to die on a cross at Calvary to reconcile sinful men and women to a Holy God. He is the only way to God, and salvation is found in no other. He is the Saviour of the world.

Those who have experienced the saving grace of Christ, who know their sins are forgiven and have been made spiritually alive by God, have thankful hearts. This short booklet is written to help Christians worship their Saviour and Lord. It uses the Scriptures to describe the wonder, glory and majesty of Jesus Christ. Glorious words and metaphors are used in the Bible to describe the Creator of the heavens and the earth, the Holy One of God. Just under two hundred biblical texts have been used to build up a word picture of Jesus – The King of Glory. All the phrases are biblical, although most are paraphrased to help with the flow of language. Scripture references are provided in a bibliography, so readers can examine the original text for themselves.

Ted Williams

Who is this King of Glory?

The Lord strong and mighty

The Lord mighty in battle

The Lord Almighty –

He is the King of Glory

Psalm 24:8,10

The radiance of God's glory

Jesus Christ is the Radiance of God's glory and the exact representation of his being
He had glory in his Father's presence before the world existed
He is the Rising Sun who came to us from heaven
He is as the Light of Morning when the sun rises, even a morning without clouds
His face is like the sun shining in all its brilliance
He is the Sun of Righteousness with healing in his wings
His eyes are as a flame of fire, and on his head are many crowns
He is the Image of the invisible God
In Him all the fullness of the Deity lives in bodily form
His name is called The Word of God
He is Pre-eminent in all things
He is Great and of great power, his understanding is infinite
He is the Alpha and the Omega, who is and who was and who is to come
He who came from heaven is above all
He is the Lord from heaven
He was in the beginning with God, and he was God

Creator of all things

Jesus Christ laid the foundations of the earth, and the heavens are the work of his hands

He made the heavens, even the highest heavens, and all their starry host, the earth and all that is on it, the seas and all that is in them

He made the earth by his power, established the world by his wisdom and by his understanding stretched out the heavens

He is the one Lord, through whom are all things and through whom we exist

He gives to all men life and breath and everything

He made all things; and without him was not anything made that was made

He is the Lord of heaven and earth, and does not live in shrines made by man

The Altogether Lovely One

Jesus is the Altogether Lovely One

He is the Lily of the Valleys, and the Rose of Sharon

He is both Root and Offspring of David

He is the Lion of the tribe of Judah

He is the Bright and Morning Star; he is the Fairest of Ten Thousand

He is the Fairest of the Sons of Men

He is the Desire of all Nations

He is the Amen, the Faithful and True Witness

He is the Beginning and the End, the First and the Last

The Beloved Son of God

Jesus is the Beloved of God
He was loved by the Father before the foundation of the world
He was made flesh and dwelt among us, full of grace and truth
He came into the world to bear witness to the truth
He is the Anointed One
He is the Mighty One of God
He is the Son of the Living God
He received honour and glory from God the Father when the voice came from the Majestic Glory saying, **"This is my beloved Son, with whom I am well pleased"**

A man of sorrows

Jesus, being in very nature God, did not consider equality with God something to be grasped
He made himself of no reputation, taking the form of a servant
He was deeply despised, abhorred by the nations
He was despised and rejected of men; a man of sorrows and acquainted with grief
He has borne our griefs and carried our sorrows
He was oppressed and afflicted, yet he opened not his mouth
He was a worm and not a man, scorned by men and despised by the people

When He was abused he did not retaliate, when he suffered he uttered no threats

He was encircled by a band of evil men; he was poured out like water

He was led as a lamb to the slaughter; he opened not his mouth

He was pierced for our transgressions

He humbled himself, and became obedient unto death – even the death of the cross

He himself bore our sins in his body on the tree

He is clothed in a robe dipped in blood

The Risen Christ

Jesus Christ is risen from the dead

He rose again the third day according to the Scriptures

He has been raised from the dead and is never to die again; death no longer is master over him

He was raised from the dead through the glory of the Father, so that we too might walk in newness of life

He was declared with power to be the Son of God by the resurrection from the dead

He entered heaven itself, now to appear in the presence of God on our behalf

He is the Living One; he was dead, and he is alive for evermore

He is the Prince of Life, the one whom God raised from the dead

Saviour of the World

Jesus is the Lamb of God who takes away the sin of the world

He has appeared, once at the end of the ages, to put away sin by the sacrifice of himself

He died for the ungodly; while we were still sinners he died for us

He loved me and gave himself for me

He made peace through the blood of his cross

He laid down his life for us

He is the atoning sacrifice for our sins

He came into the world to save sinners

He is able to save forever those who draw near to God through him

He is the One Mediator between God and men; he gave himself as a ransom for all

He is the Door. If anyone enters by him, he will be saved. Neither is there salvation in any other, for there is no other name under heaven given among men whereby we must be saved

He saved us, not because of any works of righteousness that we had done, but according to his mercy

He forgave us all our sins

He became the author of eternal salvation to all who obey him

He is our Redeemer – the Lord Almighty is his name

He is indeed the Christ, the Saviour of the world

The Light of the World

Jesus is the Light of the world
He is a Great Light seen by the people walking in darkness
He is a Light to the nations, an Everlasting Light
He was the True Light which gives light to every man coming into the world
In Him was Life, and the life was the Light of men
He has Life in himself, and he gives life to whom he will
He is the Bread of Life which came down from heaven
He is the Good Shepherd who gives his life for the sheep
Jesus is the True Vine; the branch cannot bear fruit unless it abides in him
He is the Resurrection and the Life; whoever believes in him shall never die
He is the Way and the Truth and the Life; no one comes to the Father but by him
He gave the right to become children of God, even to those who believe in his name
He came that we might have life and that we might have it more abundantly

The Lord our Righteousness

Jesus Christ is the Righteous One
His righteousness reaches to the heavens
His righteousness is like the mighty mountains
He loves righteousness and hates wickedness
His belt is righteousness, and faithfulness the sash around his waist

He was in all points tempted like we are, yet without sin
He committed no sin; no guile was found on his lips
He is just in all his ways and kind in all his doings
He has displayed his saving righteousness to all the nations
His throne is for ever and ever; a sceptre of righteousness is the sceptre of his kingdom

God's Indescribable Gift

Jesus is the same yesterday and today and for ever
He is the Author and Finisher of our faith
He is an Anchor for the Soul, both sure and steadfast
He is a Shield for all those who take refuge in him
He is the Shepherd and Guardian of our souls
He is the Great Shepherd of the sheep
He is a Friend who sticks closer than a brother
He is like the shadow of a Great Rock in a weary land
He is the Rock of my salvation; he is the Word of Life
He is the Power of God and the Wisdom of God
He is the Lord Strong and Mighty
He is the Warrior King in the cause of truth and justice
He is called Wonderful, Counsellor, the Mighty God, the Everlasting Father, the Prince of Peace
He is the same and his years shall have no end
He is the Indescribable Gift of God

The One Foundation

Jesus is the Living Stone, rejected by men, but in God's sight chosen and precious

He is a Tried Stone, a Precious Cornerstone, a Sure Foundation

He is the One Foundation; there can be no other

He is the Chief Cornerstone; in him the whole building is joined together

He purchased the Church of God with his own blood

He gave himself to purify a people of his own who are zealous for good deeds

He is the Head of the Church

He loved the Church and gave himself up for her that he might sanctify her

The Holy One of God

Jesus is holy, blameless, unstained, separated from sinners, exalted above the heavens

He is the Holy One of Israel

He entered once for all into the Holy Place by his own blood, thus securing an eternal redemption

He is a Priest forever after the order of Melchizedek

He is the Great High Priest over the house of God

He alone is Holy. All nations shall come and worship him

He is the High and Lofty One who inhabits eternity, whose name is Holy

He is the holy Lord God of Hosts, the whole earth is full of his glory

He will come again

When Jesus comes in his Glory and all the angels with him, then he will sit on his glorious throne. All nations will be gathered before him

He will appear a second time, not to deal with sin but to save those who are eagerly waiting for him

He comes to be glorified by his saints and to be marvelled at on that day among all who have believed

When Christ who is our life appears, then we will also appear with him in glory

He will come on the clouds of heaven with power and great glory

He will descend from heaven with a shout, with the voice of an archangel and with the trumpet of God; the dead in Christ will rise first

Jesus will go forth and fight against those nations as when he fights on a day of battle. On that day his feet shall stand on the Mount of Olives

He will destroy the lawless one with the brightness of his coming

Jesus will be King over the whole earth. On that day there will be One Lord, and his name the Only Name

Judge of All

Jesus will judge the world with righteousness

He is the One ordained by God to be judge of the living and the dead

He has been given authority by the Father to execute judgement; the Father judges no one, but has given all judgement to him

He is the Righteous Judge – he will award on that Day the crown of righteousness to all who have loved his appearing

He is the One Lawgiver and Judge, he who is able to save and to destroy

He is ready to judge the living and the dead

He will judge the secrets of men

He will execute judgement among the nations

He will repay every man for what he has done

He comes with ten thousands of his saints to execute judgement on all

His court will sit in judgement, and the books will be opened

He will judge the world with righteousness and the peoples with his truth

Worthy to be praised

Jesus is worthy to receive glory and honour and power for he created all things

He is the Lamb who was slain; he is worthy to receive power and riches and wisdom and strength and honour and glory and blessing

He is worthy to take the scroll and to open its seals, for he was slaughtered and by his blood he ransomed for God saints from every tribe and language and people and nation

To Him was given dominion and glory and kingdom that all peoples, nations and languages should serve him

He is the Ancient of Days, his garment is white as snow; thousands and thousands minister to him and ten thousand times ten thousand stand before him

Jesus – the name which is above every name, that at the name of Jesus every knee should bow, in heaven and on earth and under the earth

He is great and greatly to be praised; his greatness is unsearchable

He is Lord both of the dead and of the living

He is Lord of all

He is worshipped by the hosts of heaven

King of Glory

Jesus Christ is seated at the right hand of the throne of the Majesty in heaven

He is very great; he is clothed with honour and majesty

He is the King of the Jews and the King of Israel

He is the King of the nations; great and wonderful are his deeds

He is the King of Peace; he shall speak peace to the nations

He is the King of Righteousness

He is the Living King, whose name is the Lord of Hosts

He is the King of Heaven; all his works are right and his ways are just

He is far above all rule and authority and power and dominion, and above every name that is named, not only in this age but also in that which is to come

His dominion shall be from sea to sea, and from the River to the ends of the earth

He was given dominion, glory and a kingdom, that all peoples, nations and men of every language might serve him

His dominion is an everlasting dominion which will not pass away, and his kingdom the one which will not be destroyed

His kingdom is Everlasting

He is the Living God and the Everlasting King

He is the King of Kings and Lord of Lords

Jesus Christ is the King of Glory

Bow down and worship

While I live I will praise the Lord Jesus Christ
Every day I will praise you
I will praise your name for ever and ever
I will meditate on the glorious splendour of your Majesty
I will declare your greatness
I know that my Redeemer lives, and at the last he will take his stand on the earth
I myself will see Jesus with my own eyes – I, and not another
My soul yearns for you in the night, my spirit within me earnestly seeks you
I will seek him whom my soul loves
O come, let us worship and bow down; let us kneel before the Lord our Maker
Praise him for his mighty acts; praise him according to his excellent greatness
Let everything that has breath praise the Lord
To Him who sits upon the throne, and to the Lamb, be blessing and honour and glory and might for ever and ever

AMEN and AMEN

Bible References

Quotations are taken from the King James Version of the Bible unless otherwise indicated. The other translations of the Holy Bible that have been used are the Revised Standard Version (RSV); New International Version (NIV); The Revised English Bible (REB); New King James Version (NKJV); New Revised Standard Version (NRSV) and the New American Standard Bible (NAS). The initials indicate the translation that has been used. As pointed out in the foreword, many verses have been paraphrased.

The Radiance of God's Glory
Hebrews 1:3 (NIV); John 17:5 (NRSV);
Luke 1:78 (NIV); 2 Samuel 23:4;
Revelation 1:14 (NIV); Malachi 4:2;
Revelation 19:12; Colossians 1:15;
Colossians 2:9 (NIV); Revelation 19:13;
Colossians 1:18; Psalm 147:5; Revelation 1:8 (RSV);
John 3:31; 1 Corinthians 15:47; John 1:1-2.

Creator of all things
Psalm 102:25; Nehemiah 9:6 (NIV);
Jeremiah 10:12 (NRSV); 1 Corinthians 8:6 (RSV);
Acts 17:25 (RSV); John 1:3; Acts 17:24 (RSV).

The Altogether lovely One
Song of Solomon 5:16; Song of Solomon 2:1;
Revelation 22:16; Revelation 5:5;
Revelation 22:16 & Song of Solomon 5:10;
Psalm 45:2 (RSV); Haggai 2:7; Revelation 3:14;
Revelation 22:13.

The Beloved Son of God
Ephesians 1:6; John 17:24 (RSV); John 1:14;
John 18:37 (RSV); Daniel 9:25 (RSV);
Psalm 50:1 (NIV); Matthew 16:16;
2 Peter 1:17 (RSV).

A man of sorrows
Philippians 2:6 (NIV); Philippians 2:7;
Isaiah 49:7 (NRSV); Isaiah 53:3; Isaiah 53:4;
Isaiah 53:7; Psalm 22:6 (RSV); 1 Peter 2:23 (REB);
Psalm 22:16,14 (NIV); Isaiah 53:7 (NKJV);
Isaiah 53:5 (NIV); Philippians 2:8; 1 Peter 2:24 (RSV);
Revelation 19:13 (NRSV).

The Risen Christ
1 Corinthians 15:20; 1 Corinthians 15:4;
Romans 6:9 (NAS); Romans 6:4 (NAS);
Romans 1:4 (NAS); Hebrews 9:24 (RSV);
Revelation 1:18 (REB); Acts 3:15 (NAS).

Saviour of the World
John 1:29 (RSV); Hebrews 9:26 (NKJV;)
Romans 5:6,8 (NRSV); Galatians 2:20;
Colossians 1:20; 1 John 3:16; 1 John 2:2 (NIV);
1 Timothy 1:15; Hebrews 7:25 (NAS);
1 Timothy 2:5,6 (RSV); John 10:9 (NKJV) &
Acts 4:12 (NRSV); Titus 3:5 (NRSV);
Colossians 2:13 (NIV); Hebrews 5:9 (NKJV);
Isaiah 47:4 (NIV); John 4:42.

The Light of the World
John 9:5; Isaiah 9:2 (NIV); Isaiah 42:6 (RSV) &
Isaiah 60:20; John 1:9 (NKJV); John 1:4;
John 5:26,21 (RSV); John 6:41; John 10:11;
John 15:1,4 (RSV); John 11:25,26 (RSV);
John 14:6 (RSV); John 1:12 (NKJV); John 10:10.